Titles by Janvier Chouteu-Chando

The Usurper: and Other Stories
Triple Agent, Double Cross
Disciples of Fortune
The Union Moujik
Splendid Comets
Flash of the Sun
Fortune Calls
Fortune's Master
Fortune's Children
The Norilsk Bears
To Be In Love and To Be Wise
The Fire and Ice Legend
The Sweetest Madness
The Grandmothers
The Hunger Fire
The Shades of Fire
Father and Sons
The Doctors
Dark Shades
Fateful Ties
The Verdict of Hades
His Majesty's Trial
Ngoko's Folly
The Usurper
The Dowry
I am Hated
The Oaf

Non-Fiction Titles by Janvier Chouteu-Chando

THE CANARY IN A COAL MINE EFFECT:…Assassinations..
FALLEN HEROES: African Leaders Whose Assassinations…
BROKEN ENGAGEMENT: Why a Donald Trump Win…
THEIR LAST STAND: Donald Trump's Upset Victory…
Ukraine: The Tug-of-war between Russia and the West
Cameroon: The Haunted Heart of Africa

Cameroon's So-Called Opposition

Janvier Tchouteu

TISI BOOKS

NEW YORK, RALEIGH, LONDON, AMSTERDAM

PUBLISHED BY TISI BOOKS
www.tisibooks.com

ISBN-13: 978-1-7181-9306-2
ISBN-10: 1-7181-9306-8

PUBLISHED BY TISI BOOKS
www.tisibooks.com

NEW YORK, RALEIGH, LONDON, AMSTERDAM

Printed in The United States of America

EPIGRAPH

"It takes more than just today and the immediate tomorrow to carry out a fundamental change of the political system in Cameroon."

—Dr. Samuel F. Tchwenko

Acknowledgement

My deepest, warmest and everlasting thanks to Dr. Samuel F. Tchwenko and Christopher N. Chando for challenging me towards the path of humanity's enhancement.

DEDICATION

This book is dedicated to all the historic figures in Cameroon's history whose self-sacrificing commitment to the cause for a "New Cameroon" that safeguards the wellbeing, unity and happiness of Cameroonians pitted them against the local and foreign forces of darkness that have been suffocating Cameroon as a dehumanizing political system.

Cameroon's So-Called Opposition

Contents

MAPS

African Democracy Ratings

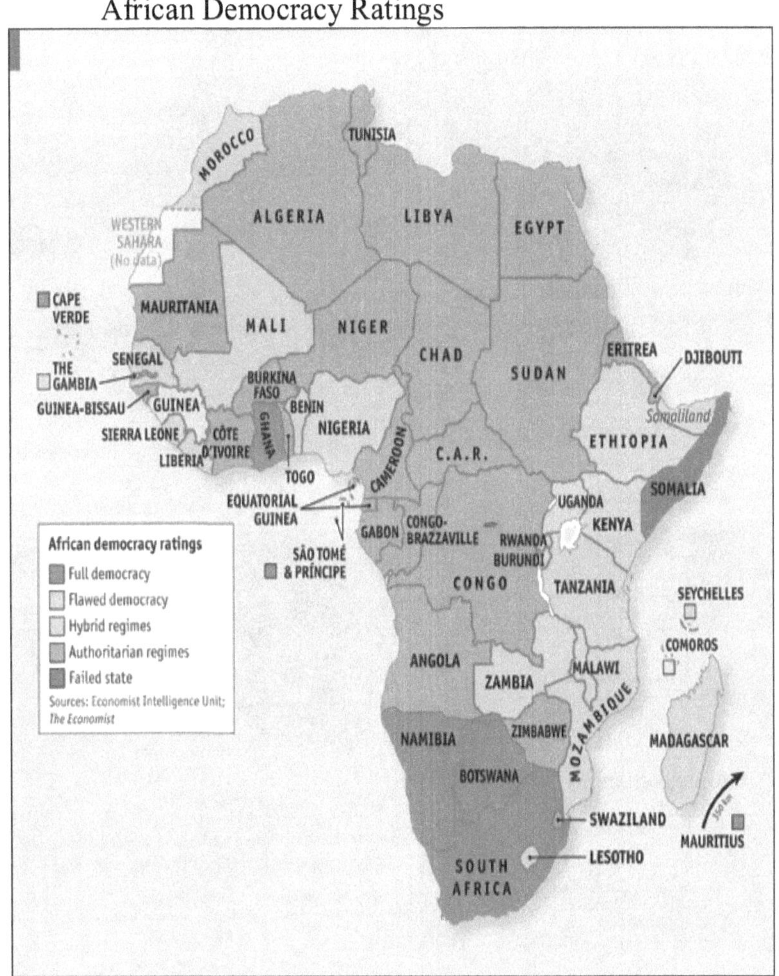

Partition Map of Africa: 1884-1914

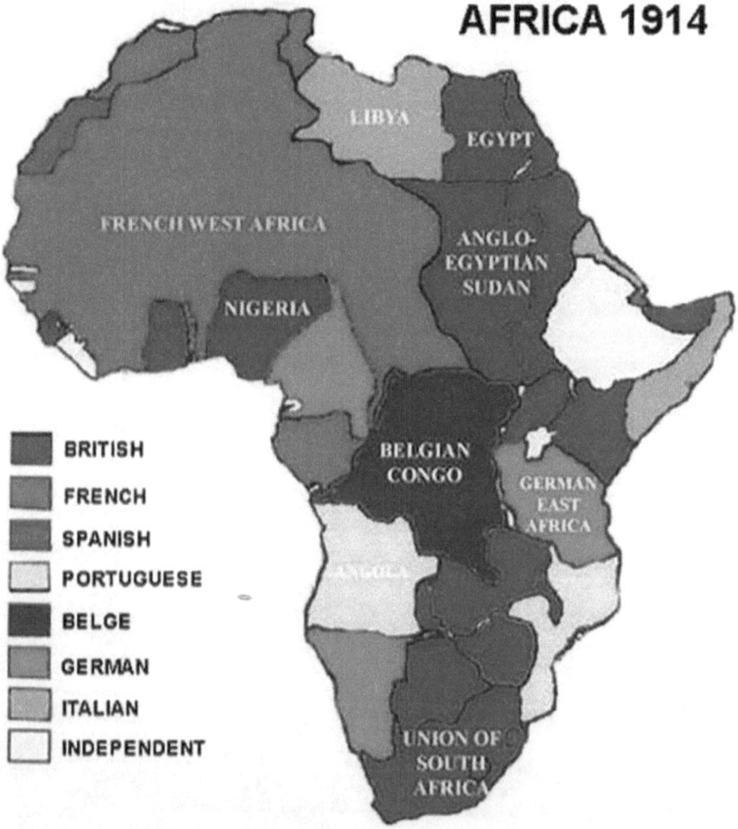

Cameroon on a map of the world

Cameroon over time

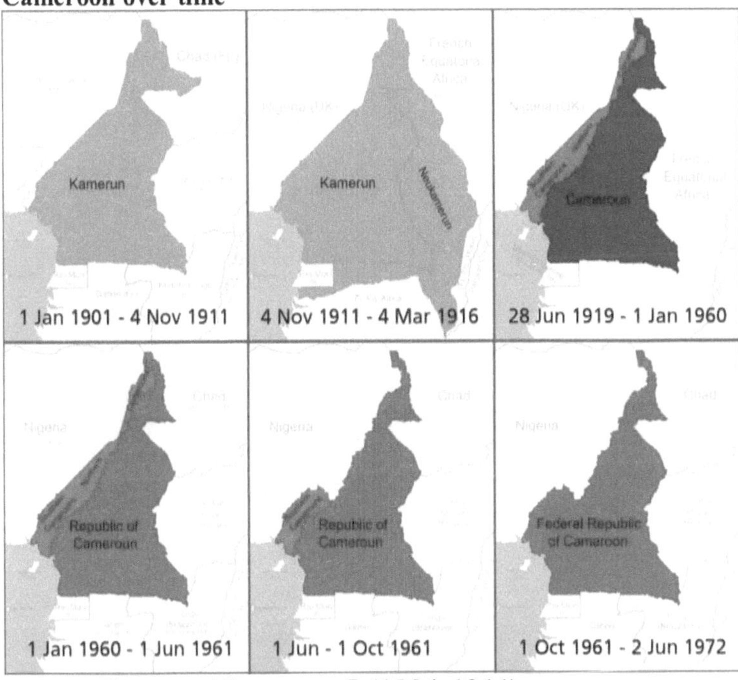

1. German Kamerun I (1884-1911)
2. German Kamerun II (1911-1916)
3. British Cameroons&French Cameroun: 1916-1960
4. British Cameroons&La Republique du Cameroun (1960-1961)
5. British Southern Cameroons&La Republique du Cameroun (1960-1961)
6. Reunited/Independent Cameroon today.

Quotes

"We are not involved in this struggle only because we think that we will dismantle this system in the course of our lives. We hope Cameroon changes tomorrow. But if it doesn't, we will be happy to know that we made the ground fertile for the next generation that will end the rot in this country, and then establish the "NEW CAMEROON".

Dr. Samuel F. Tchwenko, former UPCist and chief ideologue of the historic SDF of 1990-2002

"Cameroon is not a country of slaves that no man can free."

Janvier Chouteu-Chando

"We are in the process of creating what deserves to be called the idiot culture. Not an idiot sub-culture, which every society has bubbling beneath the surface and which can provide harmless fun; but the culture itself. For the first time, the weird and the stupid and the coarse are becoming our cultural norm, even our cultural ideal."

Carl Bernstein,

"We find that at present the human race is divided into one wise man, nine knaves, and ninety fools out of every hundred. That is, by an optimistic observer. The nine knaves assemble themselves under the banner of the most knavish among them, and become 'politicians'; the wise man stands out, because he knows himself to be hopelessly outnumbered, and devotes himself to poetry, mathematics, or philosophy; while the ninety fools plod off under the banners of the nine villains, according to fancy, into the labyrinths of chicanery, malice and warfare. It is pleasant to have command, observes Sancho Panza, even over a flock of sheep, and that is why the politicians raise their banners. It is, moreover, the same thing for the sheep whatever the banner. If it is democracy, then the nine knaves will become members of parliament; if fascism, they will become party leaders; if communism, commissars. Nothing will be different, except the name. The fools will be still fools, the knaves still leaders, the results still exploitation. As for the wise man, his lot will be much the same under any ideology. Under democracy he will be encouraged to starve to death in a garret, under fascism he will be put in a concentration camp, under communism he will be liquidated."

T.H. White

"Every great cause begins as a movement, becomes a

business, and eventually degenerates into a racket."
Eric Hoffer

"...The world gets blessed every now and then with unique souls who though burdened by thcir invisible crosses, still have the extraordinary strength to forge ahead in life and give others a helping hand at the same time. Despite their tribulations, most of us think they are fine. Even when the weight of their crosses become unbearable, even when they proceed in a breathless manner, we still have a hard time understanding that they are drowning. In fact, we even condemn them for failing to sacrifice more..."
Janvier Chouteu-Chando, Disciples of Fortune

"Blind party loyalty will be our downfall. We must
follow the truth wherever it leads."
DaShanne Stokes

If a political party does not have its foundation in the determination to advance a cause that is right and that is moral, then it is not a political party; it is merely a conspiracy to seize power.
Dwight D. Eisenhower

Chapter One

Politicians and Revolutionaries in the Struggle for the NEW CAMEROON

Politicians are not those who are meant to change a system and take a country out of an impasse into the future. That is the work of revolutionaries.

Politicians operate in established systems and do the job of politicking to defend, safeguard or promote certain interests, be they individual, group, ethnic, regional, linguistic or national, based on empty phrases or through a clearly defined thought formulation (idea or concept).

Revolutionaries, on the other hand, are those challenging a system, expecting to bring it down and institute a new system that would serve the interest of the trodden majority (the suffering or struggling masses). In the cause to bring down the system, revolutionaries do not expect to benefit or thrive from the struggle. Instead, they are prepared to sacrifice everything for the struggle.

The sad thing is that while the Cameroonian struggle to change the system is a revolutionary struggle, most of the leadership in the so-called opposition parties talk of politics and expected rewards even though they are still engaged in the struggle to change the system. That is why most of them compromised the ideals of the struggle with excuses that "it is impossible to live on clean politics as a genuine opposition in Cameroon." There are and there have been Cameroonians who selflessly gave in their worth to the struggle and felt it was dishonorable to use the struggle to achieve personal benefits. They were and are the union-nationalists and revolutionaries.

During my years of involvement in the struggle, I finally realized that the system (the Ahidjo-Biya regimes backed by the French mafia group controlling African affairs) feared and respected these revolutionaries and union-nationalists for their genuineness, unwavering nature, and integrity. But strangely enough, the politicians who profess to be in the opposition conceived a hatred for these revolutionaries and union nationalists just because these revolutionaries and union nationalists are genuine and are not like them, and because they look with horror at the deception of the politicians who are trying to live off politicking and in doing so, compromised the struggle and betrayed the aspirations of the struggling masses.

Strangely enough, we failed in this phase of the struggle (1990-2002) because politicians led the struggle to change the system (a revolutionary demand) instead of revolutionaries and union-nationalists who are far less likely to be compromised by the negative values of the anachronistic French-imposed system.

Janvier Tchouteu   *Friday, 15 April 2005*

Chapter Two

Symbiosis Among Cameroon's Famous Political Parties

Self-declared political analysts who fail to see the whole nature of things in the political arena called Cameroon easily mortify advocates of change with their parochialism and distortion of the country's reality. They fail to understand its history, the confluence of world powers over its control and fate, the force of global business entities that make a mockery of the balance of interest and values equation espoused by the countries they hail from. They even fail to understand that in Cameroon; most of the famous are the infamous.

For nine years now, since I quit the SDF that Fru Ndi's mafia had hijacked, I have been stating that Fru Ndi's SDF and the French-imposed system under Biya are in a symbiosis. They sustain each other. It is sometimes disheartening when some Cameroonian pundits (self-declared and recognized) fail to acknowledge the insightful words of Cameroonian union-nationalists and revolutionaries who were deeply involved with the SDF at all levels when the party embodied the soul of the Cameroonian struggle and carried the torch dropped by the historic UPC of Um Nyobe, Felix Moumie, Ernest

Ouandgie and Ndeh Ntumazah—patriots who put the struggle above their personal well-being, and in so doing paid a high price for it— in most of the cases, the ultimate price.

I found out from the CPDM's biggest wit in the UK in 2002, that Fru Ndi's SDF with Ngwasiri as the frontman had signed a pact with the CPDM to take the seats the regime allowed the SDF to win in the 2002 parliamentary elections, when the SDF was two days away from debating it in a NEC meeting. And of course, Fru Ndi overrode the NEC decision and sent his boys to parliament, feeding on the monthly cuts he was getting from them.

This election is the last gasp of Cameroon's political megalomaniacs, including Paul Biya. It would clearly identify the ranks and camps, that is, those who understand what the struggle is all about— those who embrace the unifying vision of THE NEW CAMEROON; those who reject the system, its custodians, its masters and its beneficiaries; those who identify, support and stand with the camp of the cheated, patriotic and struggling Cameroonian majority; those who embrace the humane forces of the world and strive to make Cameroon a part of the world of civilized nations. It would identify these genuine advocates for change from those who betrayed and are betraying Cameroon.

In a nutshell, the aftermath of this election will pit those who identify with the tenets of CAMEROONIAN UNION NATIONALISM against THE EVOLUES who sustain the system and are taking Cameroon into the abyss. The aftermath of this election would be a fight to redeem the soul of Cameroon. It would be hard and merciless for the advocates of the New Cameroon, but it would be our only salvation. And only an alliance between the soldiers of the last phase of the struggle (the post-independence generations) and the under-30s age groups, guided by the vision of the NEW CAMEROON and versed with our turbulent history, shall we be able to sweep away this evil anachronistic system and confine it to the dustbin of history.

We are less than three weeks away from a historical revelation that will change the ballgame in an arena that some of us naively call Cameroonian politics involving Paul Biya, but which in reality is the Cameroonian struggle against a Foccart-DeGaulle system installed almost seven decades ago under the guise of fighting communism, a struggle given a blind eye by the western powers who gave France a free hand in Africa. It is a struggle against a mafia setup in Cameroon and Africa that involves corrupt politicians and big businesses that espouse their interests but not the universal human values.

Janvier Tchouteu   *September 21, 2011*

Chapter Three

CAMEROONIAN OPPOSITION LEADERSHIPS:
Myths and the Future of their Parties:

Cameroon is not a country of slaves that no man can free.
All we need……

Just before the last masquerade called the 2004 presidential elections, I decided to profile the prominent so-called opposition leaders (Fru Ndi, Ndam Njoya, Bello Bouba) in the best-unbiased manner possible. The befitting title I came up with for their profiles was: "THE LAST GASP OF CAMEROON'S POLITICAL MEGALOMANIACS. I decided not to publish those profiles.

The biggest mistake made during the last phase of the struggle was to invest overwhelmingly in individuals rather than the ideal of the struggle. It was the easiest route to power, but a disaster in waiting when those individuals become powerful and lose their heads (by having delusional fantasies of wealth, power, or omnipotence). That is what happened to the above figures while in the opposition, a condition already suffered by Biya after he was given power and survived coups.

Leaders for a cause are promoted, like products. And the image makers in the early days of the SDF did a good job.

Fru Ndi, Ndam Njoya, and Bello were not the smartest in their parties, they did not confront danger more than everybody, they did not pay the highest price (lives, property, family etc) more than everybody, and they were not the major brains in the scheme for the successful expansion of their parties or the biggest contributors to the party's' ideologies. Dedicated people to the cause pushed their names to easily sell the party and to win popular support in order to assume power. The populace, unfortunately, buys the myth of the leader. It is, however, the responsibility of the new leader to balance the myth built through expectations and publicity, with reality.

But then, often in history, the leaders come to believe that the image projected of them is the reality of their true selves. And it becomes a disaster when these projected leaders are made to see and think that way by those close to them who have a vested interest in keeping them delusional. Nero, Caligula, Idi Amin, etc suffered those fates. Initially blessed with the overwhelming public support that arose from the situation at the time, these leaders often fall to the psychopathological condition characterized by delusional fantasies of wealth, power or omnipotence in their later rule.

Those who oppose these pathological egoists become targets to be rid of because they spoke contrary to the leader's wishes. In the blind quest to leave a legacy based on the myths, these political megalomaniacs end up destroying the forces (party, country, army, organization)that gave them power, wealth and omnipotence. So, is there a future for CDU? No. there is no future. It would die with Ndam Njoya. Is there a future for NUDP? No. It would die with Bello Bouba. Is there a future for SDF? The best that can come out of it after Fru Ndi is that it would be a pale shadow of its former self. And the CPDM? It would be wrecked by havoc after Biya and it is going to die the day it loses its ruling party status.

So, what is the future? Many will ask. The future is a new force built around tested advocates of change who never folded under the last phase of the struggle, and advanced representatives of the embracing ideology for the new Cameroon that embodies its union nationalism and revolutionary path.

Janvier Tchouteu   *02/13/ 2006*

Chapter Four

John Fru Ndi's Call for his supporters to risk their lives over the fake results of the 2004 presidential elections in Cameroon

I am tempted to comment on this issue of the last electoral masquerade each time I read utterances from its contestants. It was predictable even to the most stupid political novice that Biya's electoral rigging machinery (the most efficient in the world) would declare him victorious despite his less than 10% of popular support. All those who contested the election, Fru Ndi included knew that. No struggle can succeed if it fails to be scientific (taking into account statistics) and dialectic. It was also clear that by participating, the contestants would be legalizing Biya's usurpation. So, Fru Ndi continues to madden me with his cry of "foul" when he had the most favorable position against Biya and blew it(deliberately and also perhaps out of ignorance), thereby setting the true exponents of change years back in the struggle to realize a new, united, progressive, democratic and economically promising and advanced Cameroon.

We should be honest with ourselves and accept the harsh reality by asking this question. The SDF has participated in five elections and has been cheated massively in all. But how many times has Fru Ndi led the people in virulently contesting the results? The harsh answer is that only in the 1992 and 2004 presidential elections that he contested. So over the years, Fru Ndi failed to distinguish the interest of the struggle (the ideals of Cameroon's union nationalism with the fulcrum being the realization of the objectives of reunification and independence) and his personal interests (power, wealth, glory). In the struggle for the future New Cameroon, Fru Ndi, Ndam Njoya, Bello Bouba, and all the other fake opposition leaders have become irrelevant. It is time they bow out of the scene instead of being an obstacle in the struggle with their presence. They contributed enormously in keeping Cameroon at this stage of political incomprehension and lethargy.

Janvier Tchouteu   *Monday, 08 November 2004*

Chapter Five

THE POST-SDF-NUDP-CDU PHASE OF THE
STRUGGLE FOR THE NEW CAMEROON

There is something we have to recognize. The Biya regime
and the custodians of the system are the worst criminals to
the Cameroonian soul. They are thieves, liars, killers,
sadists, election riggers, discriminators, maniacs and what
not. But one thing about it all is that they know how to do
those negative acts. They are negative perfectionists.

But then, what about us? We, who oppose, resist, reject
and are trying to sweep them out of power. Do we know
how to do our job? Do we have the resilience to confront
them as they do in maintaining the status quo and the
benefits they derive from it? Only a scrupulous survivor
can defeat an unscrupulous survivor which is Biya, his
regime and the French-imposed system in Cameroon.

Some of us became involved in the struggle from its
infant days, worked in the SDF at different levels, gave in
everything without anticipating anything material in return.
By 1994, the party was acutely sick; by 1998/1999 it was a
chronic malady; and in 2002, it was terminally ill. A clique
was responsible, and those who believed in the
revolutionary objectives of the struggle— the union
nationalists who considered the purpose of the struggle to
be far above their personal interests or considerations, had

come to realize that Fru Ndi and his clique in the SDF had become an impediment to changing the system just like Bello Bouba, Ndam Njoya etc had become earlier. They too had become compromised by the negative values of the system. The Fru-Ndi led clique needed the Biya regime to thrive. And the SDF is almost dead because of them. They too betrayed the struggle. I am proud I quit the SDF in July 2002. It was like a process of self-redemption or like accepting that a church or clergy too had become corrupt and had also become an obstacle to change. It was a painful but necessary thing to do after more than a decade in the struggle and paying a heavy price for it. Thousands of other Cameroonians did the same— especially the union-nationalists with the revolutionary streak. The party's best brains and chief ideologue also quit that 2002.

I must say from my profound observation that we of the post-independence generations still have a lot of work to do, based on our thought formulations. Nevertheless, I am happy that we have taken the first step in that direction. Many of those commenting in our various forums (fore) are now talking about changing the system, unlike the pre-independence so-called opposition leaders who were talking about changing the Biya regime. That is a positive development. Fru Ndi-led SDF, Njoya-led CDU, Bouba-led NUDP etc failed because they were incapable of rising up to the challenge of confronting the depth of the Cameroonian malady(the shortcomings of the system)and of coming up with an alternative direction and values to lead Cameroonians to the change and a desirable society.

Changing the system calls for fundamental changes in ourselves. This requires rejecting all the wrong values of the system, even if it means doing so to our own detriment (economic, social and political). Such a rejection requires identifying our enemies, who in reality are those who are sustaining the system. That could be us, people in our families, personalities in our tribes or ethnic groups that we look up to, revered figures in a movement or political party that we support or even an idea that we are benefiting from. Besides the mental ability to identify the enemies, we also need the ability to identify the true friends of the people. I say so because during the third phase of the Cameroonian struggle (1990-2002) more effort was made to hunt and betray the true friends of the people (the union nationalists and revolutionaries) by the cliques holding leading positions in the so-called opposition parties than was made to confront the system and the Biya regime. And unless the true friends of the people— the union nationalists and revolutionaries lead the struggle, it becomes difficult, if not impossible to imagine that change can ever take place in Cameroon.

Janvier Tchouteu   *Tuesday, 15 February 2005*

Chapter Six

THE RETARDING INFLUENCE OF CAMEROON'S POLITICAL LUNATICS IN THE STRUGGLE TO GET RID OF THE SIX-DECADE OLD FRENCH-IMPOSED SYSTEM

Every area (village, town, district, department, region or province etc) in our country has its fair share of political lunatics; and they are a minority of the population. When most of the political lunatics support the evil system in power, it makes the job easy for exponents of change, whether at the national level or at the regional or municipal levels.

However, in those areas where this minority of political lunatics claims to be on the side of the exponents of change and not with the government, they actually become retarding elements in the cause for the "NEW CAMEROON" either because of their one-sidedness, unreliability or because of their confusion. This minority are the pseudo-opposition parties. Faced with the case of the pseudo-opposition, exponents of change should know that they have a deep problem in their hands. Unfortunately, these pseudo-opposition parties who claim to be on the side of change distract the true exponents of change (union-nationalists and revolutionaries) from focusing on the evil-French-imposed system. They, especially, mortify and demoralize the ranks of the struggling Cameroonian masses whose acceptance of the whimsical ways of the pseudo-opposition parties gets translated into political lethargy, a psycho-social state that the best of true advocates of change would have a hard time whisking them out of.

Ultimately, these political lunatics who all along have been serving the interest of the system, end up associating themselves with the system either through actions or political alliances that resuscitate the dying system or by openly embracing the ruling party of the system that they had been supporting all along, thereby becoming "PARTIES OF THE SYSTEM" in the process.

It has been observed with clarity that the major political parties in Cameroon that were identified as opposition political parties in 1990 and 1991 have today been transformed into Parties of the System by their leaders who were all members of the system's ruling party in the period before 1990, the CNU/CPDM which was the sole party in the country at the time. In taking the people—those who reject the system and advocate for a New Cameroon—for a ride in this huge deception, Cameroon's political lunatics make themselves enemies of the people and members of the conspiracy that is keeping Cameroon in political, economic and social bondage.

Janvier Tchouteu   *August 11, 2013*

Chapter Seven

JOINING THE SYSTEM IN A UNION GOVERNMENT WITH THE BIYA REGIME

Joining the Biya regime in a unity government? Madness, an absurdity to the furthest degree and treason to the patriotic objectives of the struggle. True the majority of Cameroonians want change and the struggling masses are mature in their political manifestations. But once again, they may find themselves betrayed by their political leaders who would be there for their interests only by engaging with the Biya regime.

Unfortunately, all the parties mentioned above (the current opposition) are not revolutionary and lack the far-embracing union-nationalist ideals that epitomize the struggling masses. The union nationalists in the SDF leadership quit the party when Fru Ndi and his mafia made a deal with the CPDM following the 2002 Parliamentary and Council elections. So I won't be surprised if the present Fru Ndi-led SDF completely takes off the mask and join the government. But then, it would be the final treason, and it would be the duty of Cameroonians from all regions, ethnic groups, tribes and provinces to condemn and reject them, because they too like the Biya regime would have made themselves fully as obstacles to the struggle to realize a free, united, liberal, democratic, progressive and economically promising New Cameroon

.Even so, it is about time Cameroonians identify the commitment of their leaders to the struggle to change Cameroon. Most of those mentioned fall under the category of moderates and liberals. None are union nationalists. That is why they talk of "in politics "instead of "in the struggle". Politics involves interests. Practical politics involves interest groups against one another in a functioning system (a democracy). We don't have a democracy and the struggle is about changing a system to make politicking, and hence competition possible. Changing a system is revolutionary. And the real struggle in Cameroon is changing the anachronistic French imposed system that was put in place under Ahidjo and is being maintained by the Biya regime, a system that betrayed the ideals of reunification and independence.

Janvier Tchouteu   *November 02, 2004*

Afterthought: December 29, 2010

True exponents of change have been observing the recent confidence and audacity of the Biya regime in its latest foray into the Northwest province and the humiliating posturing of known leaders from this honorable province of change, leading the struggling masses and advocates of change in the province feeling that they have been completely deserted. We have also been observing the increasing number of presidential hopefuls that make pundits to wonder if they understand what the struggle is all about. In fact, one would be tempted to borrow from Che Guevara in his observation that "the problem with Africans is incomprehension."

It is mind-boggling imagining that change can be realized in Cameroon under the current setup of a decrepit opposition, the best-rigging machinery the world has ever produced (the French imposed anachronistic system under the stewardship of Paul Biya) that disenfranchises more than half of its population before elections, prevents more than half of the registered voters from voting, ensures multiple voting for its supporters, prevents the opposition from having representatives in most of the polling booths and acts at will in multiplying the vote tallies at the booth, district, divisional, provincial(regional) and national levels. And when the election masquerade is over, France, as usual, would be there to congratulate Biya, thereby leading the international effort for the regime's legitimization.

We are about to get into the next decade of the New Millennium. The conflagration of forces, time and destiny is on the side of advocates of change. The New Cameroon would be born in this decade. But it would be a hard and merciless struggle. It would need an effective organization, dedicated leadership, a spirited population, a united purpose, a national ideal, knowledge of our history and reconciliation with our past to make the change less costly. It would involve dismantling the system. That calls for undivided ranks in the opposition. We should start 2011 by building-up resolve, clearly defining a strategy, identifying our goals and clearly identifying the camps. Indispensable in the effort are purposeful debates, progressive alliances and an effective PR.

The New Cameroon will be born on the shoulders of the post-independence generations, the *Parlement* age-group, and especially on the feet and voices of the post-1990-generation.

Janvier Tchouteu   *July 14, 2012*

Chapter Eight

On the Absence of Political/Military Cooperation Between Opponents of the Biya Regime/French-Imposed System in Both the English-Speaking and French-Speaking Regions of Cameroon

Both the English-speaking and French-speaking parts of Cameroon need to work together to get rid of this French-imposed system and found the "New Cameroon" that fired the dreams of our forefathers to the point where they died in their hundreds of thousands fighting for reunification and independence, and to the point where they campaigned and voted in their overwhelming majority in the former British Southern Cameroons for the cause to bring back together the lands of the former German Kamerun.

It is the job of those who reject the system—the political establishment dominated by its custodians who are no more than mercenaries for their French masters — to work together on a common national idea or ideal of founding the New Cameroon, explore their shared purposes and desire for a better future for all Cameroonians, a development that would once again clear all doubts, strengthen the sense of brotherhood and a common future and reiterate the understanding that this new phase of the struggle isn't intended to realize the disintegration of Cameroon, but rather to complete its unfinished liberation frozen since 1955.

We also need to realize that those who consider themselves secessionists, separatists or restorationists, are giving the Cameroonian political establishment (the French puppets/mercenaries), the pseudo-nationalists claiming to be patriots, the political elites of both the ruling party and the so-called opposition parties , the opportunity to pose as union-nationalists (civic-nationalists), the opportunity to present themselves in the eyes of Cameroonians as those engaged in a fight to keep Cameroon together, when in reality they were put in place to strangle Cameroon.

The process of founding the New Cameroon should lead to the end of Biya rule, the dismantling of the evil system and not the disintegration of Cameroon. All the progressive forces of the land should agree on that, to facilitate the creation of purposeful alliances, the setting of realistic goals, and the implementation of coherent strategies.

Janvier Tchouteu   *January 06, 2018*